# Presentation Skills Masterclass

# Want to be a Better Business Presenter?

### Business Presentations and Public Speaking

## Michael Jackson

# Preface

If you're planning on going places in business or public life, your success will largely depend on your ability to communicate well, often through the medium of presentation. Successful careers are built on great presentation skills, and opportunities have been lost by people who failed to impress when it was their turn to get up and speak.

In almost every business discipline, presentations have become the accepted format for information distribution. No one "reads the memo" these days. People show up for a meeting and expect to get the full story, on the spot, in a way that excites, interests, or simply informs. Get it right, and your reputation is enhanced, and you will be asked back for more. Get it wrong, and you may be consigned to the backbenches because you either bored the audience or failed to communicate your message.

Perfect presentations are a product of good preparation and lots of practice; even the most charismatic business people still need these elements coupled with technique and professionalism. Winging it is not an option.

Read this book, watch the videos (the links are inside), and learn the key techniques easily and quickly. You'll be shown exactly how to plan, construct, rehearse, and deliver so your messages resonate with your audience, and your ideas get enthusiasm and support every time.

# About the Author

Michael Jackson has over 30 years of strategic business, marketing, and communications experience. London educated and trained in business strategy, development, and communication, he has worked personally with leaders such as Nelson Mandela, and Richard Branson, as well as the directors of many other leading global businesses such as Microsoft, Qatar Airways, and HP.

With over 2,500 conferences under his belt, Michael is internationally regarded as a full-time professional speaker, Master of Ceremonies, and writer and has also become globally renowned and sought-after as a specialist on the subjects of trends and change within a business context.

He has carved out an enviable reputation over 15 years as one of the best business-to-business speakers and facilitators on the global professional circuit. He speaks at approximately 160 conferences and seminars each year across Africa, Asia, Europe, the USA, and the Middle East to audiences ranging from factory workers to Heads of State. He is consistently rated by his clients, conference organizers, and audiences alike as "simply outstanding" for the way he creates and delivers powerful messages and weaves personalized company and industry messages into all of his materials to suit each audience precisely.

Michael's track record includes consistently and accurately predicting changing market performances, trends, and consumer behavior for companies, industries, and markets around the world. With the hints, tips, and skills you will discover in this book, you'll be able to motivate business audiences, as he does, to get the great results you seek for yourself.

www.theothermichaeljackson.com

# Table of Contents

Preface ........................................................................ 3

Presenting And Public Speaking. It Looks Easy When It's Done Well. ................................................................... 9

Getting the Presentation Structure Right: Planning, Building & Refining............................................................22

Presentation Construction ...............................................33

What? Me Worry? ...............................................................45

8 Ways to Guarantee a Satisfied Audience. ..................55

PowerPoint & Keynote .....................................................71

Appendix: The 7-Intelligence Type Test ......................82

# 1.

## Presenting And Public Speaking. It Looks Easy When It's Done Well.

### What's Your Handicap?

*Most people approach public speaking with about as much enthusiasm as weekend golfers facing their first tee shot! Sadly, most business events set speakers up for failure before they even open their mouths.*

If you've ever played golf, you'll know the feeling.

Walking to the first tee, you feel your palms go sweaty, your throat dries up, and you begin to wonder why on earth you even agreed to play the stupid game in the first place.

Your peers are watching. There's an air of expectation, and you know it's up to you to *perform*. After selecting a club, and while trying to look as nonchalant as you can, you step up and prepare to do your best . . . At least with golf, once you're

–

beyond that first hole, it usually gets better. Presenting doesn't until, of course, you know what you're doing.

Jerry Seinfeld once quipped that when it came to a funeral, most people would prefer to be in the casket than delivering the eulogy if given the choice, and he was right.

The phobia of presentation and public speaking is so widespread today that thousands of people around the world actually earn their living by speaking professionally for organizations at corporate events and functions

Whether speaking on behalf of a company or to its customers or staff, the demand for professional business-to-business speakers is at an all-time high, and never has it been more applicable.

Our 24/7, image-driven, internet and media saturated world is simply forcing business to raise its communication standards. But it's not just public speakers that are cleaning up because of this shortfall in skills inside most companies. Even the apparently mundane treadmill of internal PowerPoints could be dramatically enhanced if everyone understood the key elements of successful presentations. When it's your job to impart knowledge and information to your work colleagues, the effects will be dramatically amplified if you do it well.

We live in a world where no one has time to read an annual report any more: where politicians have had to learn the art of the ten second "sound bite," and the cult of instant celebrity is worshipped and revered.

The mastery and use of words and pictures as well as an ability to capture and hold the imagination is now all important.

Are you fully prepared, ready, and able to stand up in this frenetically-paced, attention-deficient world and instantly

---

speak to your colleagues, staff, dealers, customers, or the media with credibility and earn their respect, trust, or admiration?

Better still, are you suitably prepared to do so? Good presenting is all about your ability to capture the audience's attention quickly and hold their interest while you deliver your message. Your objective is to paint a canvas on which they can see the big picture and their part in it.

A good presentation makes it easy for the audience, in their own minds, to create and believe the answers or outcomes that you require. This book will help you get there.

In this guide, you'll find all the theory, techniques, and activities you'll need to learn how to prepare, create, and deliver appropriate, relevant, and meaningful business presentations to any audience anywhere.

# A Question of Learning?

Sometimes called the Pyramid of Consciousness, this diagram represents each of the stages of learning that we go through on a continual basis as human beings. We all begin at the base: from a stage of unconscious incompetence.

Let's use the analogy of learning how to drive to explain this.

We all start as a child with no knowledge of the process we call driving. We need to take lessons to learn the process. This is the point where **we simply don't know what we don't know.**

We can then move to the next stage of learning where we discover that **we know what we don't know** as we become consciously aware of being incompetent!

## Pyramid of Consciousness
## Driving Skills

We now need to take the time to learn the actual process of driving, and eventually (after someone has been bold enough to offer us some lessons), we reach the stage where we can take a driving test. In other words, that's where we have to display that we are now capable of driving, and that we are consciously competent. If we can show that we are, that *we know what we know,* we will then be legally allowed to drive.

Do you remember the exact feeling you had when you actually passed your driving test? It felt great didn't it?

At the precise moment we became full-fledged and legal drivers, driving solo for the first time, we never felt more competent at anything in our lives. We were so pleased with ourselves that we wanted to tell the whole world!

That feeling of elation lasted (sadly) about two weeks, as it does with anything we've learned, and then real life took over. Without even realizing it, we slipped into the next stage where we became totally and unconsciously "competent" and started driving without thinking as if by remote control.

Then it was time for some bad habits to creep in: reading the newspaper or an iPad, making mobile phone calls, sending text messages, and even putting on makeup—all while we're engaged in the process of driving. We have reached the point of *not knowing what we know*.

Is this stage dangerous? You bet. Yet, sadly, this is the stage that virtually every individual on earth reaches and where most remain for the rest of their lives.

Few of us ever pass into the realm represented by the summit of the pyramid—where we become truly and totally *aware* and, as a result, totally competent. The odds are less than one in ten thousand people ever get there. Malcolm Gladwell, in his book *Blink,* says it takes around 10,000 hours of practice.

Everybody else spends their lives at the level just below the pinnacle: remaining unconsciously competent. ***They simply don't know what they know.***

No wonder the legendary American industrialist Andrew Carnegie said: **"Give me someone of average ability with a burning desire to succeed, and I will give you a winner in return every time."**

Sadly, the vast majority of people seem to lack this basic burning desire to continue to try and succeed; they simply quit trying after about two weeks of mastering something.

So, how does this relate to you and your presentation skills? Well, unless you are planning a career as a public speaker, it's unlikely you'll ever amass those ten thousand hours in a single lifetime. However, if you're prepared to model your approach and technique on the key success factors of those who successfully make their living this way, you should have no trouble quickly acquiring the key skills necessary to achieve a much higher level of competency and effectiveness.

In business, there are more bad presenters than good ones, so simply being better than most people is going to give you a huge advantage the next time you stand up in a meeting, conference, or boardroom anywhere. And people are going to notice and remember you and your message.

# Do You Think Like A Waiter Or A Chef?

Taking basic materials and being able to create a fantastic new meal—earning the plaudits and winning over the crowd a la Gordon Ramsay or Jamie Oliver—is exactly what we should be striving to achieve with our next (and every) presentation. Great chefs take ordinary, everyday ingredients and do something magnificent with them

Mix it up from time to time, try new things, and push yourself.

Like a great chef, take your daily ingredients, plan your recipe out in advance, time the offering to perfection, and present it in a manner that absolutely stuns the audience. Sit back afterward and watch the rave reviews roll in.

## It's Not A Boring Conference. It's Corporate Theater!

If you forget everything else you ever learned about presentations, you should never forget this: the objective of a presenter is to communicate a clear message to the audience and be certain it was received both positively and accurately.

To achieve this, you must plan everything with your audience in mind. Unless you're familiar with everyone's passions and prejudices (for example: you work together all the time), you should take a little time to research those who will be your audience. Different types of people react to different forms of stimulus, as we'll discover in a moment.

Your first job is to profile your audience and cover as many of the various preferred communication styles as you possibly can. Here's an explanation.

# Introducing Howard Gardner's "Seven Sets of Intelligence"

In the heyday of the psychometric and behaviorist eras, it was generally believed that intelligence was a single entity that was inherited, and human beings—initially a blank slate—could be trained to learn anything provided it was presented in an appropriate way.

Nowadays, an increasing number of researchers believe precisely the opposite: there exists a multitude of intelligences that are quite independent of each other; each intelligence has its own strengths and constraints; the mind is far from unencumbered at birth; and it is unexpectedly difficult to teach things that go against early "naïve" theories that challenge the natural lines of force within an intelligence and its matching domains. (Gardner 1983)

In the world of the Presenter, this psychobabble boils down to a simple mantra: it will all go a lot better if you understand who you're talking to and how they'll respond to your communication. Audiences watch, listen, and learn in very different ways.

It's the reason you had a favorite subject and a favorite teacher at school, and conversely, the reason you had a subject or two that simply didn't make sense, no matter how you tried to look at it. Gardner, an amazing psychologist, determined that all human brains are as individual as human fingerprints. They see, hear, and respond to each stimulus in varying combinations of seven different ways.

Think of an old-fashioned metal file cabinet. Remember the ones that stood in the office with a stack of metal drawers? Well, the human brain operates a bit like one of those: opening each "drawer" of its several different learning styles to a lesser or greater degree. Each of us can open all the drawers, but our brains are wired in unique ways.

The drawers in our brains are labeled for each of the following seven learning styles: linguistic (words), logic (math), rhythm (music), movement (kinesthetic), visual (image), and both intrapersonal and interpersonal abilities (the way we think of ourselves in the world and the way we think others see us).

Gardner highlighted that the teaching methodology we normally apply to children, cramming their heads with the same sets of stimuli from text books throughout their formal education period, doesn't allow for individual traits. He felt that if we could adopt a methodology for understanding each child's unique combination of learning preferences, we would achieve a great deal more with their education. Imagine if a child who wasn't strong in logic but understood rhythm was taught math in a rhythmic style; they'd probably learn math easier and achieve more with it.

We all had favorite (and least favorite) subjects at school. It's simply because our own combinations of the seven individual learning styles are so strongly ingrained in each of us. We tend to carry those preferences into the careers we choose.

Use the table to assess the likely capabilities and perceptions in terms of the mind-set of the audience members who will be attending your presentation. Your goal is to reach as many of them as possible: that means tailoring your presentation materials to appeal to as many of the learning styles as you can.

Once you consider how the audience will be listening to you and your message (and therefore, reacting and responding), you can better consider and build different elements into your presentations to ensure they ultimately get what they want. This applies to the style and type of slide deck you choose to develop, the way you move and speak, the speed and rhythm of your delivery, and even the things you actually say.

The world's best communicators manage to cover all these bases at the same time, especially when speaking to huge conference audiences.

If you want to see this in practice, being done to perfection, watch any of the speeches delivered by Presidents Clinton or Obama on YouTube. You'll be able to check off most of the common intelligence types as being addressed within the first five minutes. Model your presentations this way, and you'll reach more people, more successfully and quickly, while holding everyone's attention.

If you're interested in the huge subject of intelligence profiling, and indeed, if you would like to understand your own profile further, there is an exhausive test questionnaire in the Appendix that you may find useful in determining how your own automatic style or preference has previously dominated your thinking, and therefore, your slide development.

You must not make the mistake of assuming that everyone will "just get the message," especially if you are delivering to a range of listening and learning profiles

.

| Intelligence type | Capability & Perception | Characteristic Occupations & Vocations |
|---|---|---|
| Linguistic | words & language | Typically writers, poets, lawyers and speakers |
| Logical- Mathematical | logic & numbers | Scientists, engineers, computer experts, accountants, statisticians, researchers, analysts, traders, bankers, bookmakers, insurance brokers, negotiators, deal-makers, trouble-shooters and directors. |
| Musical | music, sound, rhythm | Musicians, singers, composers, DJ's, music producers, piano tuners, acoustic engineers, entertainers, party-planners, environmental advisors and voice coaches. |
| Bodily-Kinaesthetic | body movement control | Usually dancers, demonstrators, actors, athletes, divers, sports-people, soldiers, fire-fighters, performance artistes, oste-opaths, fishermen, drivers, crafts-people; gardeners, chefs, acupunctur-ists, healers, adventurers. |
| Spatial - Visual | images & space | Artists, designers, cartoonists, story-boarders, architects, photographers, sculptors, town-planners, visionaries, inventors, engineers, cosmetics and beauty consultants |
| Interpersonal | other people's feelings | Typically therapists, HR professionals, mediators, leaders, counsellors, politi-cians, educators, sales-people, clergy, psychologists, teachers, doctors, heal-ers, organisers, carers, advertising pro-fessionals, coaches and mentors. |
| Intrapersonal | self-awareness | Usually associated with those who are self-aware and involved in the process of changing personal thoughts, beliefs and behaviour in relation to their situa-tion, other people, their purpose and aims. Actors, inventors, politicians and authors for example. |

# 2.

# Getting the Presentation Structure Right: Planning, Building & Refining

Now that you've been thinking about the audience and the manner in which they watch, listen, and learn, its time to move on to the next stage of development. Constructing a great presentation requires three key elements before it's ready to be delivered.

First comes the *planning* stage. This is where you define the objective and the messages as well as the basic format in which you intend to work. At this stage, you should be looking to clearly map out your intended beginning, middle, and end.

Next is the *building* stage where you transcribe your material and break it down into the key parts, usually one per slide in your deck. Later, we'll examine how much information you should be showing on the screen versus how much you should communicate verbally. Less wording and more images are the professional approach.

Finally, you have your deck and your transcript, and it's time to start rehearsing and *refining*.

Hot Tip: Estimates vary, but you should work with the rule that twenty minutes of preparation time are required for every one minute of presentation time.

So for a half-hour presentation, you would expect to put in approximately ten hours to plan, build, and rehearse it. Of course, consummate presenters can take a new presentation directly to the delivery stage, and while this is where we all hope to get to in time, never, ever, look to shortcut this process.

The simplest and most effective way for you to understand the structure of the ideal presentation is to show you.

## The Challenge of Change

My keynote presentation materials, based on the concept of *The Challenge of Change*, have been presented to over 500,000 executives around the world in various formats over the last few years and never rated below "excellent" by the audiences.

For this reason, I would like you to consider it as your benchmark for understanding Presentation Planning in this section of the book. Please find somewhere quiet and watch the video of *The Challenge of Change* before you start this section of the Master Class. It's just under an hour long, and I hope you enjoy watching it as much as I enjoyed delivering it. Feel free to dip in and out of the presentation at will, but if you can, sit back and enjoy the whole thing.

After you watch the video, you'll be deconstructing it so that you can apply the techniques yourself. While you watch the video, see how many of the different intelligence types I've successfully addressed in the delivery. Use the form on the next page if you like.

To view the presentation, click this link http://tiny.cc/r80clx

Fact: A good presentation will always be designed to touch most (if not all) of the people in the room.

Let's understand how and why I developed this presentation plan in order for you to develop your next presentation better and engage everyone in the room.

What kind of people do you think this presentation best appeals to?

| Intelligence Type | Appeals to? | Which part does this and why? |
|---|---|---|
| Linguistic | ☐ Yes<br>☐ No | |
| Logical-Mathematical | ☐ Yes<br>☐ No | |
| Musical | ☐ Yes<br>☐ No | |
| Bodily & Kinaesthetic | ☐ Yes<br>☐ No | |
| Spatial - Visual | ☐ Yes<br>☐ No | |
| Interpersonal | ☐ Yes<br>☐ No | |
| Intrapersonal | ☐ Yes<br>☐ No | |

# Your Presentation Preparation Plan

It all begins with this six-step framework, which you should use for all your presentation planning. You should spend no longer than 30 minutes when doing it for yourself.

A little piece of trivia: some of the great Hollywood movie script proposals were actually written on the back of a single business card.

Use the questionnaire on page 21 to work through these six steps in turn.

If you don't have a specific presentation in mind yet, why not see if you can map out *The Challenge of Change*, which you just watched. The original six-step plan for that Presentation is on Page 22, so you can see how well you did.

## *"Give me the freedom of a tight brief." (David Ogilvie)*

I was privileged to work in my earlier advertising career with a doyen of the communication and marketing industry, one of the original "mad men" of advertising by the name of Michael Millsap. He'd won just about every advertising award on the planet by the time I met him, and on the first day of our working together, he said something profound to me: *"Jackson! All I want is the creative freedom of a very tight brief from you."*

At the time, with no idea of what that meant, I dutifully nodded, told him that was what I'd be doing, and promptly wrote it down to take home and study the meaning of what he'd asked of me.

It took several hours of thinking and pondering, and then the penny finally dropped. What he'd been saying, as a smart and strategic creative person, was that a problem that is fully understood is already half solved. I believe Millsap was a global advertising award winner, first and foremost, because he studied everything like a CSI detective, believing the answers always lie somewhere inside the scene of the crime. He felt the more you understood, the easier it became to find the solution. That principle must apply to your next (and every) presentation, just as it did to him in his own career.

Plainly put, when you plan and prepare judiciously and properly, you are greatly enhancing the likelihood of a successful outcome. Here's how to do this in a presentation sense. Using the table on Page 21, answer the six key presentation planning questions before you even begin to think of what you want to say or do. You will see that I've used the original planning sheet for *The Challenge of Change* for you to reference in this regard.

Remember, your answers to this planning process need to be concise and meaningful. Don't write a lot of information. Attempt to condense everything to the essence of what you are trying to achieve.

Question 3 is usually pre-answered for you unless it's a specific type of audience—perhaps financial people and their specific Gardner learning style—all types of people will usually be in the room.

The audience's attitudinal disposition (to be answered in question 4) is also crucial, and don't kid yourself here: no one ever woke up in the morning looking forward to your (or anyone's) next presentation. Audiences are often negatively inclined (or neutral at best), and you need to remember that your presentation has to be carefully designed to capture and engage them via their own unique learning and listening styles. It should be designed to take them from a negative or neutral position and lead them to a positive, powerful response statement that gets them to the point where they've understood your message and meaning.

Understanding the difference between these attitudinal and desired response statements becomes the clue to answering your final question of the six: *How on earth am I going to achieve this?*

Millsap would only allow the creative juices to flow once the previous questions had been carefully considered and fully answered, and I believe the secret to his (and your) career success was born from just that. A problem fully understood really is half solved.

Once you've determined your answers in this part of the process, you'll be ready to move on to the next step: drafting the framework of the actual content. Please remember that we are still a long way from actual slide development. "The meat on the bones" will come much later.

I'm often asked how long you should spend on the six-step planning process, and in all honesty, I don't believe you need to allocate more than 45 minutes to it. (The next stage, which I will later refer to as the skeleton framework, should also take an hour or so.)

Working on the GIGO (Garbage-In-Garbage-Out) principle, it should be easy to understand the value of this preparation process and how it will contribute to your successful delivery.

## Presentation Preparation Plan
### The Six-Step Framework

| | |
|---|---|
| What is this presentation all about? | |
| What do I want to achieve with my presentation? | |
| What types of people are in the audience? | |
| What are the audience's attitudinal dispositions before I even present? | |
| What do I want them to think, feel, and do as a result of my presentation? | |
| How do I intend to achieve this? | |

## Presentation Preparation Plan
### The Six-Step Framework

| | |
|---|---|
| What is this presentation all about? | Change is required in the business from all players. We're in a rut/we are changing/ we must change |
| What do I want to achieve with my presentation? | Let everyone buy-in to the concept of change and understand that change is nothing to fear (as well as not being unusual) |
| What types of people are in the audience? | All intelligence types |
| What are the audience's attitudinal dispositions before I even present? | Typically: "Not another one of these bloody boring presentations which we have to sit through, with some idiot droning on with bad slides. Do I really want to be here – no!" |
| What do I want them to think, feel and do as a result of the presentation? | "I never thought of change that way before! Man, I've already been through it so many times anyway and succeeded without even knowing. I don't want to be stuck in a rut - I see the need to change now - and I can and will be able to do it again" |
| How do I intend to achieve this? | A multi-media fun styled presentation using music as a tool of change in a non-threatening way. |

# 3.

## Presentation Construction

Think of Your Presentation like a Skeleton...

# The Head

The Head should
represent a
simple summary
of your goals and
objectives.

Refer back to it constantly
to check for direction and
purpose. Stay focused, in
order to avoid 'Mission
Creep'.

# The Spine

The Spine is
your Direction of
Travel. Each of
the Vertebrae
can represent
one slide in
your deck.

Plan one by one, ensuring you
have a Beginning, Middle, and
End in mind. Timing is
crucial - allow no more than
2.5 minutes per Vertebra,
Slide, or Key Point

# The Rib-Cage

The Ribs represent
the main points that
radiate from the Spine
of your Presentation

Add only as many
Points as you need in
order to communicate
your message. Avoid
Information Overload
or people won't
remember what you
want them to. Never
more than 3 main
points on each slide

# The Arms

The Arms bring expression, look and feel to your Presentation.

They also control Planning and Execution

# The Legs

The Legs support the whole show, and represent your Attitude. A competent presenter has balance and stability, and only goes onto the front or back foot to make a strong point.

# "The Challenge of Change" Deconstructed

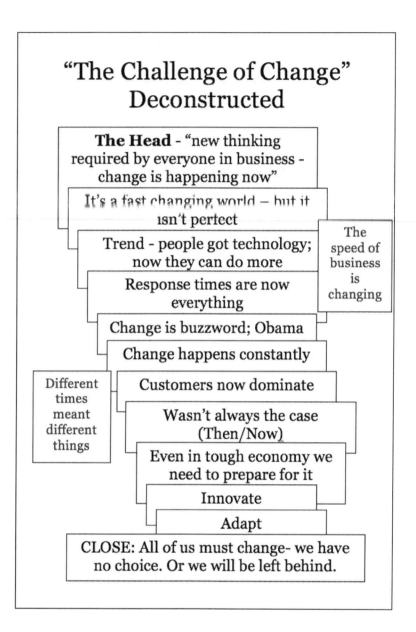

**The Head** - "new thinking required by everyone in business - change is happening now"

It's a fast changing world — but it isn't perfect

Trend - people got technology; now they can do more

The speed of business is changing

Response times are now everything

Change is buzzword; Obama

Change happens constantly

Different times meant different things

Customers now dominate

Wasn't always the case (Then/Now)

Even in tough economy we need to prepare for it

Innovate

Adapt

CLOSE: All of us must change- we have no choice. Or we will be left behind.

# "The Challenge of Change" Deconstructed

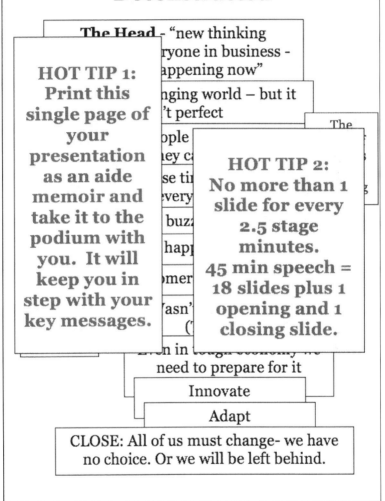

**The Head** - "new thinking
ryone in business -
ppening now"

nging world – but it
't perfect

ple
ey c
se ti
very

buz

hap

mer

asn'

**HOT TIP 1:
Print this
single page of
your
presentation
as an aide
memoir and
take it to the
podium with
you. It will
keep you in
step with your
key messages.**

**HOT TIP 2:
No more than 1
slide for every
2.5 stage
minutes.
45 min speech =
18 slides plus 1
opening and 1
closing slide.**

need to prepare for it

Innovate

Adapt

CLOSE: All of us must change- we have
no choice. Or we will be left behind.

## Summary So Far:

- Public Speaking or Business Presenting is a learned skill that anyone can master.

- It requires careful and judicious preparation, technique, and practice.

- People listen, watch, and participate in seven different ways.

- We have previously (and unconsciously) favored one or more of these styles ourselves, and have, until now, reflected this in how we present.

- A good presentation will be carefully prepared and crafted to appeal to all the intelligence styles.

- Planning every successful presentation begins with a six-step framework.

- A skeleton speech outline should be developed using simple construction techniques.

- Formatting is crucial to match time allocations.

# It's All About Confidence.

So far, so good. So how do you become comfortable in front of any audience anywhere?

I've watched globally respected executives die on stage all around the world. I've seen battle-hardened generals wither in front of an audience of soldiers, and highly revered managers lose all their credibility in less than thirty minutes in front of an audience, and not even a hostile one at that! I've also seen any number of normally genial extroverts become dry-mouthed fumblers and watched experts instantly turn into gibbering idiots. All in all, I've probably witnessed more than my fair share of corporate blood baths, most of which needn't have been as bad as they turned out to be.

Let's examine you, your state of mind, and the place you are most likely to be presenting to find out why:

## You and Your State of Mind

It's time to examine your thoughts, fears, and worries about public speaking.

What happened to you between kindergarten and today? Ask any five or six-year-old if they'd like to be in the school play and every hand goes up in the class.

By the time kids move on to high school and get asked the same question, a lot fewer hands go up, and at the college or university stage, well, there isn't a class play at all.

When and why did you lose your desire to "show and tell" or your ability to dance, sing, or act in front of people?

Take a quick test to see how reserved you are today. Quickly imagine getting into an elevator and immediately engaging in conversation with all the strangers inside as the doors begin to close. Does it seem frightening or too much? Why?

Because of societal pressures, we all grow up learning to believe in conformity. *Standing out* is often considered to be different or even abnormal, and while we all like to think that we strive for individuality, we are, in truth, most comfortable when we are part of a herd. We like to think of ourselves as being unique, but the fact is that we are a socially-conforming species and are most comfortable as adults when fitting in with a group of people who seem to be just like us.

We also possess an innate desire to be loved and wanted and not look foolish or stupid in front of people. We translate this in our business lives as not wanting to stand up and speak in front of an audience of our peers in a business presentation or conference. While we might crave unanimous acceptance and approval from others and seek it out constantly in our lives, we find ourselves all too easily embarrassed if we attempt to stand out.

So, embarrassment is a normal human trait and one that has very little to do with one's social skills or confidence levels. We instinctively find it difficult not to fear what others think of us—even when we're consciously aware that the situation doesn't matter. To increase our confidence and our willingness to "perform," we consciously need to change the way we think, and if we need to, perhaps practice "deflecting" or other relaxation techniques in order to overcome this state of mind.

The first and most important thing to remember about delivering your next presentation is that you need to present in the style and manner that *feels* comfortable and appropriate.

Secondly, you need to challenge the notion that you have to be loved or accepted by every person in your life. Sure, it's desirable, but it isn't essential. It is more important that you try to be *you*—and not just the *you* that you think other people want to see.

At five or six years old, we naturally *believe* we can sing, dance, and act. It's sad that the majority of us lose our confidence in our abilities as each year passes. We actually *can* all perform to greater or lesser degrees: we just need to be able to do it our own way—not to be judged by other people or society's standards.

So, you're free to do it your way. Be yourself and don't try to be someone you aren't. However, that doesn't mean you need to dress up like Superman and go waltzing or singing into the boardroom either!

Let's deal with the issues of relaxation and removing those nerves.

44

# 4.

## What? Me Worry?

### Glossophobia: the fear of public speaking

Feeling nervous before a speech is perfectly normal. Most speakers, even the professionals, experience what can be thought of as some degree of nervousness before presenting. Likewise, many champion athletes, rock stars, and Broadway actors feel the same thing before a game or performance. Why?

Fear is a primeval reflex to a perceived threat. It's the brain's quickest method of sharpening your essential survival senses and turning down others that aren't helpful. Unfortunately, we are still shackled by an over-reactive "fight-or-flight" chemical response that evolved over millennia to prepare us for physical conflict (fight the enemy) or exertion (run away). So it's natural to experience this state of what we call "fear" or "nervousness" in any public situation, but you need to apply "man-made" tools to combat this response because evolution hasn't caught up yet!

Every creature with a brain experiences the primeval, instinctive response to the fight or flight scenario. In fact, it's essential for survival. What happens when faced with any extraordinary stimulus is quite simple—your body issues a preparatory and instinctive command: "Prepare Yourself!" The pituitary gland responds by releasing a squirt of adrenalin into the bloodstream, and it has an instant, amazing effect.

Adrenaline makes your senses sharper and causes you to respond quicker and faster: whether to fight or take flight. Your pupils widen; your oxygen intake is increased, and as the blood courses a little faster through your system, you are better able to respond one way or the other. Imagine waking to the sight of someone breaking into your home. The same instinctive response will obviously occur, and some people will choose (in their heightened state) to stand and fight the intruder, while others are equally well-prepared and instantly equipped to run away.

Our adrenal system is important in maintaining energy levels, alertness, appropriate stress responses, and mental health as well as great athletic performance. Understanding this system helps explain that with careful consideration and some conscious thought, we are all, like great performers, able to manage that instinctive squirt of adrenaline and our response to it. I choose to use my adrenaline for good, a bit like a star athlete. I have learned to recognize this heightened state as a helpful involuntary act, not a negative one.

We can now understand the reasoning as to why some people become "nervous" at the prospect of speaking in front of a group of people. It's normal. They need to apply conscious thought to this automatic response.

At the most basic level, when unfamiliar with the situation at hand, and especially as a speaker where you are in the minority and presenting to the majority, the brain responds to the adrenal signal and tells the body that this arrangement is an unnatural or dangerous situation. However, the rational mind is capable of realizing the signaled situation is not really dangerous, and this is where you need to think of taking conscious control.

The further you ascend toward accepting and mastering this, the more likely you are to find yourself in a leadership position during your career.

## Overcoming Nervousness

So, for a presenter or speaker, nervousness is perfectly natural. It usually happens just before and during the first few moments of a speech, yet after the initial rush, most speakers forget about themselves and focus instead on their topic. After all, presenting isn't usually a life or death situation!

From here on in, a speaker will usually settle down, and their nervousness subsides. Just remember that nervousness is merely a form of energy. When properly controlled, it can be used to the speaker's advantage; it's kind of like self-hypnosis.

My good friend Rick Smith, in his book "How to Master Self-Hypnosis in a Weekend," talks about the *Line of Commitment*: an imaginary Start Line toward which you build and channel your pre-talk nerves, and when you hit the peak, you step over the line, taking all that personal energy with you.

The very best way I know to deal with nerves in the presentation context (apart from repeat – repeat – repeat) is simply to have *everything* fully prepared well in advance so you are certain there will be no malfunctions or errors from your material, your environment, or your technology.

When you have total confidence in your tools and the preparations you have made, you only have to focus on *delivery*—the important part.

## Preparation

This is, by far, the single most important step. If you haven't spent enough time preparing, there's good reason, indeed, to feel nervous. We've already covered enough preparation techniques to ensure this situation doesn't ever have to arise for you.

## Support Materials

I usually carry the single sheet of the *deconstructed presentation* with me, as previously explained. I find it helps me to get quickly back on track if I am ever distracted in any way: either by my circumstances or even a question from the audience. Audience questions are always best dealt with at the end of any presentation, and if expected or required, you have to plan time into the formatting of your presentation for them.

I'm often asked how I handle "hecklers" during a presentation, and although this doesn't occur too often, if it does arise—like a stand-up comedian would—you need to deal with the questioner firmly by telling them you'll deal with questions at the end, and then do just that.

If you are new to speaking or presenting, a series of PowerPoint slide printouts with your own notes written out is definitely the best way to go.

If you are totally sure about what you're doing, and you've mastered the technology, a tablet, such as an iPad, is a great tool. You can even present directly from the tablet if the venue has connectivity. But beware, I have seen dozens of over-complicated presentations crash because the technology went wrong on the presentation day. Don't put yourself under any additional pressure. I choose to use a reliable laptop in preference to anything else and prefer my own equipment for that very reason.

You should also consciously avoid turning to face the screen while you're talking, so if you can have a laptop screen in your forward view, this will help you stay facing the audience.

Also, and this is very important, Never EVER read a presentation. Most people make the mistake of putting too many words into every slide (I like a maximum of thirty). Reading is boredom on legs. Remember how your parents got you to fall asleep when you were a toddler? Right. They read to you!

The speed of light is faster then the speed of sound. People read twice as fast as they hear, and it's also the reason I always limit the words on each slide to a maximum of thirty. And that's a limit, not a target!

Children's storybooks were a great source of inspiration for me when I first started drawing up PowerPoint slides. Think of the old adage about a picture telling a thousand words and think of a children's book: a simple explanatory, story-filled picture with a few words used as a powerful, attention-grabbing technique employed by children's authors worldwide. It works just as effectively in the adult world too.

## Rehearsals

There is simply no substitute for a rehearsal, especially in a corporate situation. You are appearing "on stage," and you must make every effort in advance to try to familiarize yourself with the room, the venue configuration, and the expected audience makeup.

I always try to mix and mingle with people over coffee before an event and then meet them again at the door to welcome them into the room. A good look at your audience and the venue before you present will tell you a lot about them and their general attitude and can really help you relax.

It also lets your audience get close-up to you, which can warm up your relationship with them, especially if you're going to be presenting something controversial. It's a solid and dependable winning trick that I have used all over the world.

Remember, if you do well, people will want to meet you after your presentation. So why not let a few of them get a preview!

## Voice Control

It's important to be yourself and not worry about your accent or speaking style. Don't seek to change anything here, but with practice, your tone, pitch, volume, and clarity of voice can obviously be improved. Just before going on stage, try to relax your body, arms, and legs, and stand in a natural, upright position. Gentle head, neck, and shoulder stretching exercises can also help. It helps to do this in private by the way!

Some people worry that the pitch of their voice is not suited to presentations, especially when they're nervous. When someone is nervous, his or her pitch tends to be higher. Warming up the vocal chords by sipping a hot drink and exercising the voice will help to produce a lower pitch and a deeper, warmer tone.

## Be "In The Room"

Being *present* means a great deal more than just being at your presentation on time. It is essential that you are fully aware and thinking about the implications of your presentation while you engage in it. Good presentations do not happen by remote control—they happen because they are well prepared, delivered confidently, and because the speaker engages with the audience. Be warm, smile, look the part, and mirror the audience. Speaking in their style and tone settles and engages them more. Always tailor your materials to reflect your audience.

*Hot tip: When addressing an eclectic or mixed audience, tune your words to a more simplistic style. If you are addressing a multinational or multilingual audience, use "International English" and avoid complex tenses. You need everyone in the room to understand you.*

And of course, *never* try to lecture, preach, or talk down to the audience. It amazes me how many people tend to do just that when on stage, which they would never dream of doing in real life. Perhaps this is an automatic reflex, as the origins of speaking to crowds lie deep in a church style of presenting. Even the lectern you are expected to stand at has its roots in religious ceremonies. Thankfully, the modern style of presenting is seeing this archaic device being relegated to a back room as audiences better respond and engage with a confident presenter wandering up and down a boardroom or a stage. A lectern should never be used as a shield.

## Psychological Scenarios (Visualization)

Here's the thing with visualization; You either get it or you don't. However, millions of other people do get it and use it often to improve their performance. With a little light work, which simply involves relaxing and focusing on a single scenario, you can use visualization as a very effective tool to control your nerves.

Experiment with these three common scenarios.

### The Bag of Nerves

About half an hour before you get up to give the presentation, let yourself get as nervous as possible— letting it all out, so to speak. Then, rein in all these feelings and visualize yourself putting them into a big bag and tying it up or zipping it closed. Then say to yourself over and over "I've gotten rid of all my nerves. They're closed up in that bag, and they will not affect me today."

## The Most Dismal, Embarrassing Performance Ever

In this scenario, think about a particularly embarrassing event in your life, reflecting on how bad and awful it was. Then focus on how you got through it, what you learned from it, and how it is never going to happen to you again. Working from this point, visualize how successful your presentation will be and that you have nothing to be nervous about.

## Psyche Up

Develop a mantra that you can say to yourself over and over again. The most common mantras include: "I can, and I will do this," "There's nothing to fear," "I'm fully prepared, fully practiced, and I'll be great." I've watched widely respected professionals do similar things before appearing on a stage, and it's nothing to feel embarrassed about.

If you're interested in developing your visualization and self-control skills quickly, I recommend "How to Master Self-Hypnosis in a Weekend" by Rick Smith. There is a link to the book's Amazon page at the end.

No one wants a speaker to fail. It's tough enough to be seated in a darkened conference room and told to listen and learn— hardly a convenient and comfortable situation for most people without having to suffer through poor or unprofessional speakers as well.

---

Audiences are usually there for one of five reasons:

*Communication*

*Collaboration*

*Climate Audit*

*Change*

*Celebration*

And there are two distinct types of audiences in each category:

- Those who came of their own choice
- Those who are obliged to be there

You may be on stage for quite a while, so unless you look like a film star, you'd better be interesting and well prepared!

# 5.

## 8 Ways to Guarantee a Satisfied Audience.

Here's what most audiences really want. They'll judge your presentation and the validity of the messages by how many of these boxes you can check.

1. A presenter who is interested in them as unique human beings and who involves them as equals.

2. To listen according to their preferred learning style and at their own pace.

3. To get involved in a climate where they themselves feel engaged.

4. Recognition of their own experience. Their experience should be used as a resource.

5. To be able to see the relevance and application of what is presented.

---

6. Open and honest communication.

7. A dialogue that recognizes both emotional and intellectual dimensions so they enjoy the presentation and use it as an opportunity for growth.

8. Storytelling rather than advice.

What audiences don't want (among other things):

1 Presenters who are trying to be perfect or seeking approval.

2. A focus on how brilliant the presenter thinks he/she is.

3. A comedian who isn't funny.

4. Too much content crammed into too little time or bad and illegible slides.

5. Someone who reads to them or walks in front of the screen.

6. Other people's copied materials.

7. Lack of speaker preparation.

8. Discomfort: listening to a monotone voice or watching a speaker fidget.

## What a Meeting Really Is:

Let's focus on the environment where most people will do the bulk of their presenting: a Meeting or Boardroom.

Meetings come in all shapes and sizes. There are the usual office meetings, board meetings, internal seminars—all the way up to company conventions: the big one that can make or break careers, friendships, and even marriages. No stress then!

And presentations are often more than simply face-to-face events: online conferencing, *gotomeeting*, webinars, and a host of other teleconferencing systems make meetings easier to arrange than ever, so we have more of them.

Did you ever hear anyone say, "Hey, we need to have more meetings" (unless you work in France, that is)? There are more than enough meetings and with good reason. Love them or hate them, meetings are more important than ever. Modern workplaces are built on teams, the sharing of ideas, and effective project coordination, and meetings are the key components of these activities. Collaboration is the name of the game.

If communication is the lifeblood of any organization, then meetings are the heart and mind. The place where we communicate our ideas, hash them out, and share our passion for better or worse as well as develop new understandings and new directions. It's where deals are made and lost: where strategy is sliced open and examined. It's all about people *meeting* with people.

Survey results published by the Annenberg School of Communications at UCLA and the University of Minnesota's Training & Development Research Center show that executives spend on average 40%-50% of their working hours in business meetings. Surveyed professionals also believe that as much as 50% of all meeting time is unproductive, and that up to 25% of all meeting time is spent discussing irrelevant issues. They needed a survey to tell them that?

Typically, people complain that meetings are too long, scheduled without adequate time to prepare, and end without any clear result. Most of us have been to seminars or conferences where we've left feeling inspired and rejuvenated. But how many of us have ever left business meetings feeling the same way? The reason is simple; seminars and conferences are organized precisely to engage us, and meetings usually come up short on planning and preparation.

Beyond the basic inability of many people to present well in public, I've observed that a lack of diligence and care in preparation and execution of the events themselves have caused more presentation disasters than mediocre or poor speakers.

Just as a golf course needs to be controlled and managed, every staged event needs to be similarly and properly set.

## Controlling Your Environment

As with all things, the devil is in the detail. Unless you are presenting in familiar surroundings, such as your own company's meeting room, you may be working in an unfamiliar (and even hostile) environment. Never assume anything. One tiny missing element can completely derail your well-prepared presentation. Check everything you can, and where you can't, make sure you have a backup plan in case you don't find what you're expecting.

One golden rule is that you should never open any presentation with an apology, so it's your personal responsibility to ensure that, once you stand up, you have everything in place to enable a smooth performance with no technical glitches.

A professional approach, once again, requires attention in three chronological areas: Preparation, Facilitation, and Follow Up.

# 1. Preparation

## The Brief

Ensure you understand the required outcome according to the meeting organizer. Find out who will be in the audience, their titles, and if possible, their contact details for later.

## Timing of Talk

Never run overtime. Stick to your nominated time slot, especially if you are one of a number of speakers or presenters on the agenda. You may have more to say, but if you disrupt the schedule, that is what people will remember, not your content.

## Details of Venue

Where, when, and how do you get there? Never risk showing up late.

## Required Arrival Time

If you are fitting into a program, try to arrive at least an hour before rehearsal/presentation times.

## Rehearsal Time

Familiarization with the room is an absolute must. If you need to go there the day before, do so. If you have been allocated an organized rehearsal slot, don't ignore it. Even the Rolling Stones do a sound check!

## Laptop and Battery/Power Cords

Wherever possible, insist on your own laptop every time, and always take the Power Supply even if you think it's fully charged because strange things happen. It's a good idea to carry a separate extension cord, especially if you are presenting somewhere unusual where there won't be any AV support.

If you can't use your own laptop, you must make sure your presentation (whether sent in advance or brought on a flash drive) runs smoothly on the kit that's provided. Are the meeting organizers running the same version of PowerPoint or Keynote as you? If not, your slides could jump or transition badly. Don't accept "it'll be fine," because usually, it won't be.

## Projector and Power Cords

Make sure your laptop connects to the projector cable, especially if you are using mini HDMI interfaces on a MacBook or Ultrabook. It's a good idea to carry a roll of cellophane tape or some small rubber bands in case the projector connection isn't tight. Many boardrooms have very short laptop/projector cables, often at the wrong end of the room. If you make a lot of presentations, equip yourself with a small essential cable set, so you're ready for anything. It'll cost you less than $30 to put this together, but you'll never be caught out again.

## Spell Check the Presentation

Twice. And read it while you are doing it! If you are using special words, trade terms, or names in your deck, these will be from your Custom Dictionary, so be prepared and know that any computer that isn't yours will show spelling errors in draft view.

## Logo Check the Presentation

If you are presenting at a public event, you should always clear the use of Logos and Trademarks well in advance with their appropriate owners.

## Backup Presentations

Carry at least one USB flash drive with your presentation on it and make sure it's stored in the cloud somewhere accessible like Dropbox. If you suffer an equipment failure, at least you'll still be able to present on another machine.

## Use of Sound/Video and Copyright Material

In public presentation environments, only use materials that are legally obtained and licensed, such as externally-sourced illustrations, designs, icons, photographs, audio clips, and video clips. Just about everything is protected by copyright, and you may face penalties for unauthorized use.

## Embedded Media Files

Ensure that any AV materials are properly embedded into the presentation prior to screening and that original source materials are stored locally with your presentation. The cloud isn't perfect yet and using links to externally located information runs a high risk of failure.

Unless you have thoroughly rehearsed, avoid using embedded web clips that require a live internet connection, especially YouTube videos. Chances are your audience will be left staring at the blue screen of death while you frantically try to trigger your clips.

---

## Presenter Mouse

If you are using your own equipment, invest in a wireless presenter mouse. Targus, Logitech, and Kensington are the best sellers. Expect to pay around $25-$35 for a good one, preferably with an integrated laser pointer. Avoid buying one that requires software to be installed. Most of the above models start working as soon as you plug them into a USB port.

## Your Introduction

Make sure the meeting organizer or MC has your Speaker Introduction document well in advance and always take a printed copy with you (in case the MC goes sick on the day). Keep it brief. Here's a sample of mine:

> *Our guest speaker is a globally sought-after speaker on the subject of Change.*
>
> *Over the last 15 years, he has addressed over 2,500 conferences across Europe, the Middle East, Asia, the USA, and Southern Africa to audiences ranging from factory workers to Heads of State.*
>
> *Former South African President Nelson Mandela has called him "a national treasure," and he's worked personally with many leading personalities and companies around the world.*
>
> *We're delighted to have him address us today . . . so please join me in welcoming—the other Michael Jackson.*

Here's a more typical corporate one you could modify:

> *"Diana Jones is from the IT Department where she is a qualified storage expert. Her*

*presentation today concerns the implementation of our brand new storage architecture, which will benefit us all and save us time, effort, and money."*

## Clothing

The phrase here is "business appropriate." For any business presentation, you should wear the customary business attire for wherever you are. At a minimum, a collared shirt and pressed trousers. Unless you're Simon Cowell, your shirt should never have more than one open button; most men look better in a tie. Women presenters should never show cleavage, or that's all the audience will remember.

No sandals, jeans, shorts, or t-shirts should ever be worn—even at informal events; your audience may be dressed down, but you should never risk it. Only Steve Jobs ever got away with presenting in faded blue jeans and a turtleneck sweater.

## 2. On-The-Day Facilitation

This section is all about handling the room, the general environment, and anything else that might be an impact on your presentation on the day.

### The Agenda

How does the schedule of speakers run? Is there time between speakers to allow for a switchover of technology and a brief introduction of who you are? If not, can you ask for access to the meeting room and set up in advance? Are there sufficient comfort breaks (people cannot go much over two hours without a comfort break)?

### Speech Length

You should try to use a visible clock or timer. A good mouse presenter, as mentioned earlier, will include a backward counting timer that you can set as an aide. Mine, a Logitech, buzzes gently with three minutes to go and more violently at the end of the allocated time.

Looking at your watch is unprofessional as it looks to the audience like you're bored or don't know your timing, so arrange something in your sight line. Overrunning is a serious offense and must be avoided at all costs. It impacts the audience, the other speakers, the caterers, the event organizers, and is very bad form. Similarly, underrunning can cause a crisis if the next speaker isn't ready to start early.

### Room Temperature

It is not always possible to set an ambient temperature due to central or poor air conditioning. If you have some control, always set the room for several degrees lower than normal. I try and aim to get the room to a comfortable 21°C (70°F). The audience's body heat will raise the temperature to a more ambient, but not unpleasant level. If the room is too warm, you may find people getting drowsy during your presentation, especially if you are on straight after lunch. It isn't called the "graveyard shift" for nothing.

## Sound Systems

You will need sound amplification for anything over 50 people. If it's available, always use it. Lapel microphones and throat (*lavaliere* or "Madonna" style) microphones are always preferable to handheld ones. If a handheld mic is the only one available, hold it very close to your mouth to avoid popping sounds. Remember, too, that if you are wearing a lapel microphone and you swing your head to either side, the sound may fade, and it might appear to the audience that you are "off mic." Using a microphone looks simple, and it should be as long as you pay attention to your technique.

## Lighting

For large presentations, particularly theater style, lighting is critical. There needs to be enough light for the audience to see you clearly but not too much that it washes over the screen (dulling any projected images). If necessary, unscrew light bulbs that cause problems and replace them later. Do not simply assume lighting needs to be either on or off. Think about the nature of your room and use the available lighting for maximum effect.

## Technicians

Meet them, greet them, work with them (remember their names), and thank them afterwards. They are the lifeblood of every large event and can make or break your presentation.

## Stage Decking (Podium)

For anything over 50 people in the audience, you ideally need to be raised above floor level so the audience can see you clearly. And NEVER stand in front of the projector screen.

## Cabling (the Spaghetti)

Always carry a roll of duct tape and tape down all cables. Otherwise, you will trip—guaranteed!

## Safe Delete of Materials

If using a laptop other than your own, remember to safe delete your material before leaving.

# 3. Action and Reaction

## Audience Makeup and Guest Lists

Get to see, study, and think about the audience. It is essential to know who is in the room and the audience makeup by gender, type, level of knowledge, and skill sets. These are all important elements for you to gauge your own delivery style, speed, and language. Let common sense prevail.

## Flexibility in Approach

Other than arriving well in advance (which also helps with preparation of the room/surroundings), you need to be prepared to be flexible with the arrangements. Other speakers may run overtime (Grrr!) forcing you to shorten your presentation by five or ten minutes. I normally have a couple of slides that I am prepared to hide in my presentations.

## Where to Stand

There is no hard-and-fast rule for this. The worst presenters tend to "white-knuckle" the lectern; some walk and talk, while others stand alone and proud on center stage, which is the more modern approach to presenting. I normally reposition any lectern to the side and rear of the stage, and I use it only for my backup sheet and a place to store drinking water. If presenting in a meeting room or around a boardroom table, I prefer to walk around and engage the audience.

## Executive Summary

Depending on the forum and the audience, you may want to provide an executive summary for your delegates. Keep it brief, perhaps using your deconstructed

Presentation sheet as the basis. Unless you are presenting a data-heavy pitch, I would advise against giving out copies of your slides in advance because people will race ahead of you and make judgments about your material rather than the whole presentation. Always make sure you put your contact details on any papers you distribute and add a little copyright statement, for example, © 2015 Michael Jackson. It won't stop anyone from distributing your information (which can be useful for follow-up business), but it will make them think twice before they use it in their own documents or presentations.

**Evaluation Form**

If the conference or event organizers don't provide one, you should have your own drawn up and be prepared to distribute it. We all need a reality check (or to feel the love in the room) once in a while.

# 6.

## PowerPoint & Keynote

Very few of us actually have the ability to walk out on stage and present completely cold. Then again, you also rarely see actors walk onto a stage and deliver a straight monologue, especially without the use of some form of visual aid (perhaps a skull). I use PowerPoint for this reason. The Apple alternative is Keynote, and there are other software presenters available. For the purpose of this section, we can consider them all the same. Many people today disrespect and talk down the use of PowerPoint; however, I love it and will always champion its cause as long as it is used correctly.

PowerPoint can help in any number of ways. When I walk and talk on stage, I often use a so-called "comfort" monitor positioned toward me center stage as an aide-memoir of where I am in the presentation. A carefully positioned laptop linked to your presenter mouse does a similar job and is also essential if you are trying to sequence audio and imagery. You can replicate this in any boardroom or company presentation with a little advanced planning.

*"Death by PowerPoint"* is what we all despise and rightly so. Let's examine how to avoid this, and most of the other PowerPoint pitfalls with twenty-two important PowerPoint tips and hints:

## 1. Master Slide

Choose a common Master Slide look and feel with a solid background color. Use the slide master feature in the PowerPoint program. Think about the text size that you will use depending on the screen you will be presenting on and the distance of the farthest people in the audience.

## 2. Consistency and Color

Use contrasting but consistent colors in your slide build. The more contrast in your colors, the better they will display, so think logically and don't use colors that "wash out" like yellows or pale on white colors.

White backgrounds with black text are very common—easy to read—but DULL. Never use a white slide background if you're projecting onto a wall; every blemish will show up brightly on all your slides. Don't use too many colors either: usually two or three at most in a whole presentation. Remember, projection rooms are never truly dark enough, so make sure your choice stands out even in a dimly lit room.

### 3. Think Musically

Slides should flow into one another. The presentation should work as a whole unit, and you should try not to jolt your audience with slides that don't naturally follow on from each other.

### 4. Use One Central Style and Feel

Never copy and paste slides from different sources. It looks sloppy, and your audience will think you are lazy or unprofessional. Wherever you get your content or data, the presentation should belong to *you*.

### 5. Pictures

Should be sourced and used properly from a site like fotolia.com or shutterstock.com. Never use clip art. Photos are so much more professional and can be used to illustrate points, scenarios, and even feelings if chosen well.

### 6. Fonts

Fonts must be easy to read (I use Calibri) and be of a good size, taking into consideration the screen size and the audience distance.

### 7. Word Count

As a general rule, a slide shouldn't contain more than thirty words in total. I never use bullet points. It makes the flow of reading uncomfortable, and besides, everyone else does. I personally think bullets kill people!

## 8. Company Logos

You may use company logos (your own or others) by permission or credit but don't overload your slides with these elements.

## 9. Company C.I.

Your company may have a corporate instruction or Corporate Identity style guide governing the use of templates and logos in presentations. Check and implement this if it exists. Do not try to create your own standard because "you felt like it."

As much as it may pain you to use the standard template, especially if it's unimaginative or boring, it could be a career-defining moment if you choose to step outside convention. That's a risk that outweighs any potential benefit you might gain by daring to be different.

## 10. No Bar Charts or "Golf Course Graphics"

I have never seen an audience be inspired by numbers on a graph or chart (and no one ever remembers them). Find new exciting ways to highlight trends or numbers if you need them. Think big, bright, and bold—death to the pie chart or graph!

## 11. Build Slides

Look for and use the custom animation feature in the program—sparingly. It's under *Animations > Custom Animation* on the PowerPoint toolbar.

Take some time to experiment with the *slide build* feature. Never reveal a whole slide that has several points all at once. Rather use the build feature (in custom animation) to allow each point to appear one after the other as you click through the slide. PowerPoint and

Keynote have hundreds of combinations to enhance your slides. To see how they look and learn how to do them, check out some of the hundreds of PowerPoint videos on YouTube.

Custom animation should be used to transition one slide or point into the next. Dancing icons should be banned along with cartoons and funny ad clips that never have any relevance and detract from your core message. If you want to show advertising, get a job in advertising.

## 12. Headings

A good slide should demonstrate its own meaning and purpose. Headings are a cheat sheet designed by Microsoft to keep mundane speakers on track. Instead, refer to your development skeleton chart on the lectern. Children's books never have headings in them: just a great picture and a few words. The audience should primarily be following you with your slides as a simple and easy to follow (not read) device to keep the flow all together.

## 13. Sentences

Short and concise or even none at all. Try using single keywords on your slides to reference the context and as an anchor to each point you will make verbally. The objective is to have the audience look at you and listen to what you say, not to be reading and potentially misinterpreting your messages from your slides.

## 14. Opening Slide (Title Slide)

Ensure it is punchy, direct, and to the point. This is where you need to remember that if you don't get your audience to follow you in the first 2½ minutes, no matter what follows, you've lost them for good. Your opening slide doesn't need to be a mind dump of information or content either: think of a movie title and develop your material accordingly. Go back and look at my opening slide on the video.

## 15. Your Second Slide

It has to be engaging. You need to catch the audience here and carry them with you. If you fail, you may lose them for the rest of your presentation. You generally have around two more minutes to make an impression at this stage.

I never use an Agenda slide. Why waste valuable and informative time telling the audience what you are going to tell them? Just cut to the chase!

I am also not a big fan of humor and "*let me tell you the one about...*" icebreakers. If you want to be a comedian, go to a stand-up club. Instead, look to develop a relevant, killer opening that just focuses the attention on you and your material.

## 16. "Hide Slide" Feature

Go to the multi slide PowerPoint presentation view and right click on any slide layout. You will see the option to click to hide that particular slide: note it will not show, but it will also not be deleted from the slide deck.

Many presenters prepare too many slides, or they have to cut the size of the deck to squeeze into a shorter time slot. Others like to have all their backup material on slides, interspersed with the actual presentation deck so that they have data available in the right place if a particularly important question arises.

Use this feature for your own purposes. It's surprisingly useful.

## 17. Dates and Times on Slides

I've rarely seen the point of this. Sure, put the date on your Title Slide if you wish. It may be useful in the future. But on each individual slide, it's just a distraction from the core material. I have a feeling most people put it there simply because the function exists, not because it serves any useful purpose. Save your presentation decks on your hard drive with a title and put the date in there. No one else really needs to see it.

## 18. Speaker Notes on PowerPoint Template

Forget even trying to use this feature! It was designed by a non-presenter and will only assist in confusing you and focusing your attention on the laptop screen when it ought to be on your audience.

## 19. Never Walk Across the Screen

Before you present, walk the stage: see where the projection light falls and mark the points on the floor where your shadow (or your body) would block the audience's view of the screen. Blocking the screen or shadowing is a mortal sin for a presenter.

## 20. Button B (or Button W)

In full presentation mode, hit either B or W on the keyboard and the whole screen will Black or White out. Tapping the spacebar (or any other key) will bring the presentation right back. Button B is useful when you need to walk in front of the screen, or if you want to get the audience's attention away from your slides for any reason.

## 21. Keep It Simple

The KISS principle. Remember, your audience does not need to be bombarded, and your slides are there usually only as an aide-memoir to your actual talk.

## 22. NEVER EVER Read Your Slides

There. I've mentioned this again. You cannot speak as fast as a human eye can read. Reading slides (or from notes) is a sleep-inducing, brain-freezing, turn-off to your audience.

And remember, if you don't have me in the first two minutes, you have probably lost me for good.

## Finally . . .

Let's go back to that first tee on the golf course. Just as you wouldn't expect to send a novice out on the course to play a four ball with your top customers, a business should not ask a non-speaker or ill-prepared one to step up to the plate at a business event.

We live in a world where, regrettably, only first place counts, and in an environment where you only get one chance to make that impression, you have to be totally comfortable and prepared before you go anywhere near the stage.

By implementing and referring back to the content of this book, you will be better able to master both of these essential elements.

Practice makes perfect and that means you have to take it on.

*"The more I practice, the luckier I get."* Gary Player

Good luck!

And if you have any comments or queries, feel free to email me. I'd love to hear from you!

Enjoy your next presentation, and remember, a good speech can even send people into war with a positive attitude!

michael@theothermichaeljackson.com

**If you enjoyed the book, please leave a review on Amazon! The more people we can reach, the fewer boring presentations we'll all have to sit through in the future!**

# About the Author

Michael Jackson has over 30 years of strategic business, marketing, and communications experience. London educated and trained in business strategy, development, and communication, he has worked personally with leaders such as Nelson Mandela, and Richard Branson, as well as the directors of many other leading global businesses such as Microsoft, Qatar Airways, and HP.

With over 2,500 conferences under his belt, Michael is internationally regarded as a full-time professional speaker, Master of Ceremonies, and writer and has also become globally renowned and sought-after as a specialist on the subjects of trends and change within a business context.

He has carved out an enviable reputation over 15 years as one of the best business-to-business speakers and facilitators on the global professional circuit. He speaks at approximately 160 conferences and seminars each year across Africa, Asia, Europe, the USA, and the Middle East to audiences ranging from factory workers to Heads of State. He is consistently rated by his clients, conference organizers, and audiences alike as "simply outstanding" for the way he creates and delivers powerful messages and weaves personalized company and industry messages into all of his materials to suit each audience precisely.

Michael' track record includes consistently and accurately predicting changing market performances, trends, and consumer behavior for companies, industries, and markets around the world. With the hints, tips, and skills you will discover in this book, you'll be able to motivate business audiences, as he does, to get the great results you seek for yourself.

# Appendix:
# The 7-Intelligence Type Test

The more you *know yourself,* the better equipped you are to play to your strengths, not only as a presenter, but in every aspect of your life

Use the following questionnaire to score yourself for each of the seven types. You should then be able to work out your natural advantages, and use them to focus your performance.

Don't take more than a few seconds for each question. There are no 'don't know' options in the answers, so you need to take quick decisions about which option best suits your make up.

Have fun with it; you might be surprised at what you discover about yourself!

# 1: Linguistic Intelligence

| 1 | I often use stories or metaphors in order to explain something. | Yes/No |
|---|---|---|
| 2 | I like debating in discussions. | Yes/No |
| 3 | I enjoy writing stories, poetry, legends, or articles. | Yes/No |
| 4 | I would like to write a script for a play or a movie. | Yes/No |
| 5 | I like telling stories. | Yes/No |
| 6 | I like describing events in detail. | Yes/No |
| 7 | I like giving presentations. | Yes/No |
| 8 | I enjoy playing word and information games, like Scrabble and Trivial Pursuit | Yes/No |
| 9 | I like writing/typing journal entries. | Yes/No |
| 10 | I would love to create a talk show program for radio or TV. | Yes/No |
| 11 | I enjoy writing newsletters. | Yes/No |
| 12 | I love using encyclopedias, reference books, and thesauruses to expand my knowledge. | Yes/No |
| 13 | I like inventing catchy slogans, mottos, or sayings. | Yes/No |
| 14 | I like (or would enjoy) conducting interviews. | Yes/No |

| 15 | I enjoy talking and I always have something to say. | Yes/No |
|----|----|----|
| 16 | Reading is very important to me. | Yes/No |
| 17 | I usually ask a lot of questions | Yes/No |
| 18 | I hear words in my head as I listen to someone, or when I am watching TV. | Yes/No |
| 19 | I am good at spelling. | Yes/No |
| 20 | I have all round general knowledge. | Yes/No |
| 21 | I would rather listen to the radio or a audiobook than watch TV. | Yes/No |
| 22 | In discussion, I am often the leader. | Yes/No |
| 23 | I enjoy entertaining myself and others with tongue twisters, puns and nonsense rhymes. | Yes/No |
| 24 | I like to use complex vocabulary and long sentences. | Yes/No |
| 25 | When travelling, I pay more attention to signs than scenery. | Yes/No |
| 26 | I use e-mail and SMS a lot. | Yes/No |
| 27 | I prefer subjects like History, Literature, and Languages to Math, Science and Computer studies. | Yes/No |
| 28 | In a conversation, I refer a lot to what I have read or heard. | Yes/No |
| 29 | I would enjoy writing a novel or short story. | Yes/No |
| 30 | I form words in my head before I speak or write. | Yes/No |

# 2: Logical/Mathematical Intelligence

| 1 | A mathematical formula 'speaks' to me. | Yes/No |
|---|---|---|
| 2 | I see patterns in numbers. | Yes/No |
| 3 | I like experiments. | Yes/No |
| 4 | I like creating strategy games like Survivor, and treasure hunts. | Yes/No |
| 5 | I enjoy organizing my time. | Yes/No |
| 6 | I enjoy analyzing and interpreting data. | Yes/No |
| 7 | I like hypothesizing and asking *"what if?"* | Yes/No |
| 8 | I like categorizing or collating facts and information. | Yes/No |
| 9 | I like describing symmetry and balance. | Yes/No |
| 10 | I can always see the advantages and disadvantages of a situation. | Yes/No |
| 11 | I enjoy planning. | Yes/No |
| 12 | I enjoy reasoning things out. | Yes/No |
| 13 | I like playing with numbers and doing complex mathematical calculations. | Yes/No |
| 14 | I like using technology. | Yes/No |
| 15 | My favorite school subjects were Science, Math, and/or Computer Science. | Yes/No |

| 16 | I enjoy computer games. | Yes/No |
|---|---|---|
| 17 | I enjoy brainteasers. | Yes/No |
| 18 | I can easily calculate numbers in my head. | Yes/No |
| 19 | I enjoy logical games, like chess and card games. | Yes/No |
| 20 | I enjoy solving problems. | Yes/No |
| 21 | I enjoy "what if?' games. | Yes/No |
| 22 | My mind automatically searches for patterns and logical sequences. | Yes/No |
| 23 | I like rational or scientific explanations for things. | Yes/No |
| 24 | I often think in abstract concepts. | Yes/No |
| 25 | I understand and need order. | Yes/No |
| 26 | I am immediately aware of logical flaws in someone's argument or conversation. | Yes/No |
| 27 | I enjoy building puzzles. | Yes/No |
| 28 | I notice illogical sequences in (for example) events or films. | Yes/No |
| 29 | I love questioning and experimenting. | Yes/No |
| 30 | I'm interested in new developments in science and technology. | Yes/No |

# 3: Visual/Spatial Intelligence

| 1 | I think in three dimensions. I can mentally move or manipulate objects in space to see how they will interact, such as gears turning parts of a machine. | Yes/No |
|---|---|---|
| 2 | I like to produce and can easily understand graphic information, for example, using graphs or charts to explain concepts. | Yes/No |
| 3 | I can easily read a road map. | Yes/No |
| 4 | I have good special awareness; for example driving, especially parking or maneuvering. | Yes/No |
| 5 | I like building puzzles, particularly big ones. | Yes/No |
| 6 | I like creating photo collages and scrapbooks. | Yes/No |
| 7 | I like to use a whiteboard or flipchart when I am explaining something, or lecturing or teaching. | Yes/No |
| 8 | I enjoy creating videos of special occasions. | Yes/No |
| 9 | I like designing posters, murals, websites, or bulletin boards. | Yes/No |
| 10 | I find myself visualizing a lot, especially when I am listening and trying to understand. | Yes/No |

| 11 | I can easily remember large chunks of information just from reading about them. | Yes/No |
|----|------|------|
| 12 | I like creating complex 'architecture' type drawings. | Yes/No |
| 13 | I would love to make a film or a TV ad. | Yes/No |
| 14 | I naturally color code, for example, Sunday is white and Monday is red. | Yes/No |
| 15 | I find it easier to learn when I can see and observe the process. | Yes/No |
| 16 | I find it easy to see things – both concrete and linguistic – in different ways or from new perspectives. | Yes/No |
| 17 | I like building blocks, origami objects, Lego, models, and bridges. | Yes/No |
| 18 | I regularly have vivid dreams. | Yes/No |
| 19 | I like and am competent at producing art, such as illustrations, drawings, sketches, paintings, or sculpture. | Yes/No |
| 20 | I like board games like Monopoly and Trivial Pursuit. | Yes/No |

| 21 | I like using technology, such as computers. | Yes/No |
|----|---------------------------------------------|--------|
| 22 | I like to do presentations, and lecture or teach using computers. | Yes/No |
| 23 | I like creating PowerPoint or Keynote presentations | Yes/No |
| 24 | I see visual images of what I am thinking or hearing when I close my eyes. | Yes/No |
| 25 | I appreciate and notice variation in color, size, and shape; for example, I notice the colors, furniture, and interior design in rooms. | Yes/No |
| 26 | I can easily find my way around and only need visit a place once to be able to find my way back again. | Yes/No |
| 27 | I like doodling, especially when on the phone or listening to a lecture where I have to concentrate. | Yes/No |
| 28 | I prefer not to look at a lecturer's face when I am trying to concentrate, as this distracts me. | Yes/No |
| 29 | I often use visual images as an aid to recall vivid information. | Yes/No |
| 30 | I can easily fold paper into a complex shape and visualize its new form. | Yes/No |

# 4: Musical Intelligence

| | | |
|---|---|---|
| 1 | I can read body language. | Yes/No |
| 2 | I find it easy to pick up the nuances in someone's speech, for example, whether he or she is sarcastic, angry, irritated, or worried. | Yes/No |
| 3 | I enjoy music and often find myself needing it in a learning or study situation. | Yes/No |
| 4 | I will often create my own rhythm if I can't hear music, especially when I am concentrating. | Yes/No |
| 5 | I fell able to interpret what a composer is communicating through music. | Yes/No |
| 6 | I find myself responding to music by moving in time to it. | Yes/No |
| 7 | Music and singing make me feel emotional. | Yes/No |
| 8 | I find the role music plays in human life fascinating. | Yes/No |
| 9 | I collect different types of music. | Yes/No |
| 10 | I can sing. | Yes/No |
| 11 | I can 'see' music in my head | Yes/No |
| 12 | I like to analyze and critique musical selections. | Yes/No |
| 13 | I remember the words of songs. | Yes/No |
| 14 | I often have intuitive hunches. | Yes/No |

| 15 | I can 'read' people easily. | Yes/No |
|---|---|---|
| 16 | I am sometimes cynical. | Yes/No |
| 17 | I find myself listening and responding to a variety of sounds, including the human voice or sounds like nature and music. | Yes/No |
| 18 | I recognize different types of musical styles, genres, and cultural variations. | Yes/No |
| 19 | If I watch gymnastics, ballet, or sport, I can 'hear' music in the body movements. | Yes/No |
| 20 | I have a desire to create, or I have made a musical instrument. | Yes/No |
| 21 | I play one or more instruments. | Yes/No |
| 22 | I like musical games, for example karaoke. | Yes/No |
| 23 | I often tap or hum while working or learning something new. | Yes/No |
| 24 | I find myself responding to music by humming along. | Yes/No |
| 25 | I like music. | Yes/No |
| 26 | I like whistling, and often do. | Yes/No |
| 27 | I can hear a song once or twice and then sing most of it. | Yes/No |
| 28 | I can easily 'read between the lines'. | Yes/No |
| 29 | I am not easily misled. | Yes/No |

# 5: Kinesthetic Intelligence

| | | |
|---|---|---|
| 1 | I need to explore a new environment through touch and movement. | Yes/No |
| 2 | I like to touch or handle what I need to learn; I cannot just look at it. | Yes/No |
| 3 | I consider myself to be coordinated. | Yes/No |
| 4 | I like craft, like pottery or woodcarving. | Yes/No |
| 5 | I have a good sense of timing when it comes to physical activities. | Yes/No |
| 6 | I have good ball skills and can play ball games and sports. | Yes/No |
| 7 | I love movement and sport, but I'm not that proficient in any particular sport. | Yes/No |
| 8 | I enjoy participating in plays. | Yes/No |
| 9 | I prefer individual to group sports. | Yes/No |
| 10 | I like making models | Yes/No |
| 11 | I am good at sewing. | Yes/No |
| 12 | I am aware of my physical health; I exercise and eat a healthy diet. | Yes/No |
| 13 | I enjoy participating in a group activity that involves a coordinated sequence of movements, such as aerobics. | Yes/No |
| 14 | I notice when someone doesn't color coordinate their outfit well. | Yes/No |
| 15 | I really enjoy watching sport – live or on TV – and appreciate the skill involved. | Yes/No |
| 16 | I am good at arranging furniture in a room, or ornamental displays. | Yes/No |

| 17 | I have a good sense of timing in life, for example, I am always punctual and can manage my time. | Yes/No |
|---|---|---|
| 18 | I enjoy field trips, like visiting a museum or a planetarium. | Yes/No |
| 19 | I like using hand and body movements when I am talking. | Yes/No |
| 20 | I enjoy physical strategy games, like stuck in the mud and treasure hunts. | Yes/No |
| 21 | I have excellent hand-eye coordination. | Yes/No |
| 22 | I find it difficult to sit still for long periods of time, especially in a classroom or theatre. | Yes/No |
| 23 | I enjoy swimming. | Yes/No |
| 24 | I run for exercise. | Yes/No |
| 25 | I take part in marathons and fun-runs. | Yes/No |
| 26 | I am a keen and competent cyclist. | Yes/No |
| 27 | I like symmetry in a room, for example, putting two identical pot plants on either side of a couch. | Yes/No |
| 28 | I find it easy to create new forms in a sport, for example, a new type of dance, or a new version of basketball. | Yes/No |
| 29 | I often feel compelled to move about in order to keep my concentration. | Yes/No |
| 30 | I find that I need to move in some way when I am learning and building memory. | Yes/No |

# 6: Interpersonal Intelligence

| 1 | I need people around me a lot. | Yes/No |
|---|---|---|
| 2 | I am very good at mediating. | Yes/No |
| 3 | I keep strong friendships for many years. | Yes/No |
| 4 | I recognize that there are many different to communicate with others. | Yes/No |
| 5 | I make use of these different ways of communicating. | Yes/No |
| 6 | I thrive on attention. | Yes/No |
| 7 | I can often perceive the thoughts and feelings of others. | Yes/No |
| 8 | I find it easy to counsel and guide people. | Yes/No |
| 9 | People tend to come to me for counseling and advice. | Yes/No |
| 10 | I like to influence the opinions or actions of others. | Yes/No |
| 11 | I enjoy participating in collaborative efforts. | Yes/No |
| 12 | I am able to assume various roles in a group – from a follower to the leader. | Yes/No |
| 13 | I prefer to lead rather than follow. | Yes/No |
| 14 | I am quick to understand the verbal and non-verbal communication of a group or person. | Yes/No |
| 15 | I communicate effectively, both on a non-verbal and a verbal level. | Yes/No |

| 16 | I form friendships easily. | Yes/No |
|---|---|---|
| 17 | I enjoy coaching people. | Yes/No |
| 18 | I find it easy to tune into the needs of others. | Yes/No |
| 19 | I can easily adapt my behavior and conversation to different groups and environments. | Yes/No |
| 20 | I am good at organizing others to get a group project done. | Yes/No |
| 21 | I like to be needed. | Yes/No |
| 22 | I can easily work with people from diverse age groups and backgrounds. | Yes/No |
| 23 | I am a good leader and visionary. | Yes/No |
| 24 | I am good at managing people, in terms of action planning and getting things done. | Yes/No |
| 25 | I am good at arguing a point and am convincing. | Yes/No |
| 26 | I am good at handling management conflict. | Yes/No |
| 27 | I am a good 'solution-finder'. | Yes/No |
| 28 | I like to generate many perspectives on topics. | Yes/No |
| 29 | I am easily able to adapt my explanation, communication, or behavior, based on the feedback of others. | Yes/No |

# 7: Intrapersonal Intelligence

| 1 | I am aware of my emotions. | Yes/No |
|---|---|---|
| 2 | I am easily able to express how I feel. | Yes/No |
| 3 | I can find different ways to express my emotions and thoughts. | Yes/No |
| 4 | I can sit quietly for hours on my own, thinking and sorting things out in my mind. | Yes/No |
| 5 | I believe I am very well balanced. | Yes/No |
| 6 | I can work independently. | Yes/No |
| 7 | I am highly organized. | Yes/No |
| 8 | I am motivated to set goals for myself and achieve them. | Yes/No |
| 9 | I don't need people around me all the time. | Yes/No |
| 10 | I prefer to be on my own to being in a group. | Yes/No |
| 11 | I enjoy my own company. | Yes/No |
| 12 | I am very curious about the deep issues of life, and love to ponder on their meaning and relevance. | Yes/No |
| 13 | I am challenged by the purpose of life. | Yes/No |
| 14 | It is important for me to understand my inner experiences. | Yes/No |
| 15 | Human rights issues are close to my heart. | Yes/No |

| 16 | I am affected by the plight of others. | Yes/No |
|----|----------------------------------------|--------|
| 17 | I am determined to make a difference in the world. | Yes/No |
| 18 | I have a desire to empower others. | Yes/No |
| 19 | I find it very easy to consider another person's problem and to advise them. | Yes/No |
| 20 | I love to philosophize. | Yes/No |
| 21 | I am a very good listener. | Yes/No |
| 22 | I only offer advice if asked. | Yes/No |
| 23 | I never impose my ideas on others even though I always have an opinion. | Yes/No |
| 24 | I have insight into issues, and life in general. | Yes/No |
| 25 | I love writing journal entries. | Yes/No |
| 26 | I prefer to work alone. | Yes/No |
| 27 | I find it easy to tune into the needs of others. | Yes/No |
| 28 | I enjoy receiving feedback on my efforts. | Yes/No |
| 29 | I often have opinions that set me apart from the crowd. | Yes/No |
| 30 | I prefer self-directed learning, such as distance learning. | Yes/No |

# Scoring the Profile Questionnaire:

Add the number of 'yes' answers for each Intelligence as your score, then divide by 30 and multiply by 100 to get your percentage score for each Intelligence.

| Intelligence type | Score | % | |
|---|---|---|---|
| Linguistic | | | Typically writers, poets, lawyers and speakers. |
| Logical-Mathematical | | | Scientists, engineers, computer experts, accountants, statisticians. |
| Musical | | | Musicians, singers, composers, DJ's, music producers, piano tuners. |
| Bodily-Kinaesthetic | | | Dancers, demonstrators, actors, athletes, divers, sports-people, soldiers. |
| Spatial - Visual | | | Artists, designers, cartoonists, story-boarders, architects, photographers, sculptors. |
| Interpersonal | | | Typically therapists, HR professionals, mediators, leaders, counsellors, politicians, educators, sales-people, clergy. |
| Intrapersonal | | | Usually associated with those who are self-aware and involved in the process of changing personal thoughts, beliefs and behaviour in relation to their situation. |

| Intelligence type | Capability & Perception | Characteristic Occupations & Vocations |
|---|---|---|
| Linguistic | words & language | Typically writers, poets, lawyers and speakers |
| Logical-Mathematical | logic & numbers | Scientists, engineers, computer experts, accountants, statisticians, researchers, analysts, traders, bankers, bookmakers, insurance brokers, negotiators, deal-makers, trouble-shooters and directors. |
| Musical | music, sound, rhythm | Musicians, singers, composers, DJ's, music producers, piano tuners, acoustic engineers, entertainers, party-planners, environmental advisors and voice coaches. |
| Bodily-Kinaesthetic | body movement control | Usually dancers, demonstrators, actors, athletes, divers, sports-people, soldiers, fire-fighters, performance artistes, oste-opaths, fishermen, drivers, crafts-people; gardeners, chefs, acupunctur-ists, healers, adventurers. |
| Spatial - Visual | images & space | Artists, designers, cartoonists, story-boarders, architects, photographers, sculptors, town-planners, visionaries, inventors, engineers, cosmetics and beauty consultants |
| Interpersonal | other people's feelings | Typically therapists, HR professionals, mediators, leaders, counsellors, politi-cians, educators, sales-people, clergy, psychologists, teachers, doctors, heal-ers, organisers, carers, advertising pro-fessionals, coaches and mentors. |
| Intrapersonal | self-awareness | Usually associated with those who are self-aware and involved in the process of changing personal thoughts, beliefs and behaviour in relation to their situa-tion, other people, their purpose and aims. Actors, inventors, politicians and authors for example. |

Made in the USA
Middletown, DE
22 August 2017